INSIDE THE NBA

NEW YORK KNICKS

BY ANTHONY K. HEWSON

SportsZone
An Imprint of Abdo Publishing
abdobooks.com

abdobooks.com

Published by Abdo Publishing, a division of ABDO, PO Box 398166, Minneapolis, Minnesota 55439. Copyright © 2023 by Abdo Consulting Group, Inc. International copyrights reserved in all countries. No part of this book may be reproduced in any form without written permission from the publisher. SportsZone™ is a trademark and logo of Abdo Publishing.

Printed in the United States of America, North Mankato, Minnesota.
052022
092022

Cover Photo: Sarah Stier/Getty Images Sport/Getty Images
Interior Photos: Melinda Nagy/Shutterstock Images, 1; Sarah Stier/Getty Images Sport/Getty Images, 4, 12; Angela Weiss/AFP/Getty Images, 7; Emilee Chinn/Getty Images Sport/Getty Images, 8; Todd Kirkland/Getty Images Sport/Getty Images, 10; Wendell Cruz/Pool USA Today Sports/AP Images, 13; Hy Peskin Archive/Getty Images, 14; R.H. Finn/AP Images, 17; Dan Farrell/New York Daily News Archive/Getty Images, 19, 34; Bruce Bennett Studios/Getty Images Studios/Getty Images, 20; Todd Warshaw/Allsport/Getty Images Sport/Getty Images, 21; Vaughn Ridley/Getty Images Sport/Getty Images, 23; Robert Kradin/AP Images, 24; Focus On Sport/Getty Images, 27; Focus On Sport/Getty Images Sport/Getty Images, 29, 30; Jim MacIsaac/Getty Images Sport/Getty Images, 31; Jared C. Tilton/Getty Images Sport/Getty Images, 33; Rhona Wise/AFP/Getty Images, 37; Keith Torrie/New York Daily News Archive/Getty Images, 38; Steve Russell/Toronto Star/Getty Images, 41

Editor: Charlie Beattie
Series Designer: Joshua Olson

Library of Congress Control Number: 2021951663

Publisher's Cataloging-in-Publication Data

Names: Hewson, Anthony K., author.
Title: New York Knicks / by Anthony K. Hewson
Description: Minneapolis, Minnesota: Abdo Publishing, 2023 | Series: Inside the NBA | Includes online resources and index.
Identifiers: ISBN 9781532198373 (lib. bdg.) | ISBN 9781098272029 (ebook)
Subjects: LCSH: New York Knickerbockers (Basketball team)--Juvenile literature. | Basketball--Juvenile literature. | Professional sports--Juvenile literature. | Sports franchises--Juvenile literature.
Classification: DDC 796.32364--dc23

TABLE OF CONTENTS

CHAPTER ONE
BACK ON BROADWAY 4

CHAPTER TWO
NEW YORK ORIGINALS 14

CHAPTER THREE
BIG APPLE BALLERS 24

CHAPTER FOUR
NEW YORK MOMENTS 34

TIMELINE 42
TEAM FACTS 44
TEAM TRIVIA 45
GLOSSARY 46
MORE INFORMATION 47
ONLINE RESOURCES 47
INDEX 48
ABOUT THE AUTHOR 48

CHAPTER ONE

BACK ON BROADWAY

The New York Knicks finished the job on the last day of the 2020–21 regular season. In a matchup of two of the National Basketball Association's (NBA's) oldest teams, they held off the Boston Celtics 96–92. It was a significant win. The Knicks entered the day tied with the Atlanta Hawks for the fourth spot in the Eastern Conference standings. New York's win secured that position. When the playoffs opened a week later, the Hawks would have to come to Manhattan for Game 1. It's a place no visiting team likes playing.

Madison Square Garden is one of the centerpieces of New York City. It sits right on top of Penn Station, a hub of the city's bustling transit system. Over the years, Madison Square Garden has hosted famous boxing matches, political conventions, the Stanley Cup Final, and concerts by the most famous musicians of all time.

Knicks forward Julius Randle set new career highs of 24.1 points and 6.0 assists during the 2020–21 season.

However, Madison Square Garden is most famous for basketball. Since the late 1930s, it has hosted the finals of the men's college National Invitational Tournament (NIT). Winning the event was once considered a better prize than today's March Madness. Basketball superstars have graced its floor in top high school, college, and NBA games.

NEW YORK STATE OF MIND

New York City has a special relationship with basketball. From the famous playgrounds in the city to its powerhouse public high schools and several colleges, basketball is played everywhere. New York is the hometown to some of the most famous players of all time. And the New Yorkers who don't play are often passionate fans.

Since the late 1940s, those fans have met at "the Garden" to cheer on the New York Knicks. During the team's most successful periods, it was a fearsome place to play. The always-rowdy New York fans prided themselves on making life very difficult for opposing star players. At times the pressure has caused opponents to wilt. Other times it has brought out the best in the game's greatest performers. The idea of having a big game there has created many legendary "Garden Nights" through the years.

However, entering the 2020–21 season, those nights seemed like a distant memory for most Knicks fans. In the 21 years

When full, Madison Square Garden is one of the loudest arenas in the NBA.

since last reaching the NBA Finals, the Knicks had made it to the playoffs only six times. In only one of those years did they advance past the second round. And New York had not made the playoffs at all since 2012–13. During that stretch, the Knicks had often brought in high-priced stars. Then the suffering fans watched those players fail to deliver.

To make matters worse, the COVID-19 pandemic hit in March 2020. Fans were forced out of arenas nationwide for more than a year. When the teams came back to start the 2020–21 season, they played mostly to empty seats.

Randle, *left*, and guard RJ Barrett, *right*, paced the Knicks' offense during the team's bounce-back season in 2020–21.

KNICKS FEVER

On February 23, 2021, a crowd of 1,981 fans watched the Knicks lose to the Golden State Warriors at the Garden. It was far below the arena's capacity of 20,000. But it was the first time the Knicks had played in front of fans in months. The loss dropped New York to 15–17, still good enough for fifth in the Eastern Conference.

Led by young stars like forward Julius Randle and guard RJ Barrett, the Knicks were fighting for a playoff spot. First-year head coach Tom Thibodeau guided them to wins in their next three games. But then the inconsistent team hit a rough patch. The Knicks lost five of six and slipped to eighth place.

A triple-double from Randle led the Knicks to an overtime win over the Memphis Grizzlies on April 9. It was the start of a nine-game winning streak, the team's longest run of wins since New York's last playoff season in 2012–13. By the time it was over, the Knicks were well on their way back to the postseason.

JEERS AND CHEERS

When the regular season ended, the surprising Knicks were 41–31. New York's first playoff game against the Hawks was at home. COVID-19 crowd restrictions around the country were being lifted. More than 15,000 fans were allowed into the Garden to watch the opener.

While it wasn't full capacity, there were enough people to give the Knicks a home-court edge. Knicks fans showed up with a Hawks target in mind. Atlanta guard Trae Young was in his third season. A budding superstar with great shooting range, Young was the Hawks' main weapon. That made him the top priority for New York's hecklers.

From the opening minute, the fans shouted at Young. Famous filmmaker Spike Lee led the charge. The award-winning director was also a Knicks superfan. He had been sitting courtside at the Garden for more than three decades. In the

Film director Spike Lee has long been a diehard Knicks fan.

1990s the Knicks were a regular playoff team. Every year, Lee drew headlines for his verbal battles with superstars like Michael Jordan and Scottie Pippen of the Chicago Bulls. Lee was once blamed for the Knicks' losing a playoff game when his taunting fired up Indiana Pacers' star Reggie Miller. Now he went to work on Young. The Atlanta guard shrugged off the jeers. He had 11 points and six assists in the first half as the Hawks took a two-point lead into the locker room.

The game stayed close into the final moments. Young floated in a go-ahead shot with 0.9 seconds left to break a 105–105 tie. The Atlanta star held his finger to his lips to shush the crowd. For the first time all day, the Garden was silent.

BOUNCING BACK

After the Game 1 loss, Thibodeau knew his team needed to step it up. "Having fans is great," the Knicks' coach said after the game. "But we've got to play better."

It didn't seem like his young team had heard the message early in Game 2. The Hawks raced to a 57–44 halftime lead behind Young's 20 points. Randle shot 0-for-6 in the first half and scored just two.

However, Randle bounced back after the break. The day before, he had been named the league's Most Improved Player. In the second half he showed why with 13 points, five rebounds, and three assists. The burly 6-foot-8-inch forward drew a roaring reaction when he gave the Knicks a 74–72 lead late in the third quarter.

Randle's big half, and a team-high 26 points from veteran guard Derrick Rose, led New York to a 101–92 victory. The Knicks

Dibs on Thibs

Tom Thibodeau won his second career Coach of the Year Award in 2020–21. Thibodeau was the first Knicks head coach to win since Pat Riley in 1993. Thibodeau was known for coaching great defensive teams. The Knicks had the seventeenth-worst record in points allowed and the sixteenth-worst record in opponent shooting percentage in 2019–20. In 2020–21 they had the league's best record in both stats.

Veteran guard Derrick Rose joined the Knicks in a February 2021 trade with the Detroit Pistons.

walked off the floor to thunderous cheers.

It was New York's only win of the series. Atlanta came back to Madison Square Garden for Game 5 and finished off the Knicks. Young wrapped up the show by bowing to the still-jeering New York fans after hitting his last shot of the game.

Even though the Knicks' run was over, New York fans had plenty to shout about. And they hoped their young team would return to the playoffs for years to come. Randle was sure they would. Asked to sum up his feelings after the series, he stated, "We'll be back."

Randle's performance in Game 2 helped the Knicks win a playoff game for the first time in eight years.

CHAPTER TWO

NEW YORK ORIGINALS

Basketball was on the rise in the 1940s. The men's college game was gaining in popularity, especially in the Northeast. But there was no professional league in that area at the time. New York sportswriter Max Kase thought he could change that.

Kase called several arena owners to a meeting in New York City in June 1946. Along with Boston businessman Walter Brown, he pitched the idea of a new professional basketball league. Later that year, the Basketball Association of America (BAA) was born.

Kase wanted to own the league's New York team himself. But a man named Ned Irish owned Madison Square Garden, the city's most obvious home for a pro basketball team. The arena's rules said any team that played there had to be owned by Irish. So Kase went back to sportswriting while Irish got the team.

Knicks forward Harry Gallatin (11) looks to pass in a game against the Rochester Royals.

The World's Most Famous Arena

The Knicks have played their home games in Madison Square Garden since the team was founded in 1946. But the building they play in now is not the same Garden. The current Garden is actually the fourth building to carry that name. The first was built in 1879. Today's arena features a "Walk of Fame." In addition to numerous sports stars, the Walk honors several musicians who have played famous shows at the Garden, including Elton John and the Rolling Stones.

Irish's new team needed a name. He wanted something that would fit the city. When New York was settled by Dutch immigrants in the 1600s, the settlers wore pants that came just below the knee. They were called "Knickerbockers." Through the years, it had become a nickname for people who lived in New York. It was a perfect fit for the team.

Knickerbockers, often shortened to just "Knicks," was what the team was called when it took the court for the first game in BAA history later that year.

A NEW LEAGUE

The BAA wasn't the only league trying to make pro basketball happen. The National Basketball League (NBL) had been formed in 1937 in the Midwest. By 1949, however, it was struggling. Team owners from the two leagues got together and merged in time for the 1949–50 season. The new league was called the National Basketball Association (NBA). It had 17 teams, including the New York Knicks.

The Knicks were successful from the start. Under head coach Joe Lapchick, they finished 40–28 in their first NBA season. But they fell in the Eastern Division finals to the Syracuse Nationals. A year later, the Knicks went a step further. They beat the Nationals and reached the NBA Finals. There they quickly fell behind 3–0 to the Rochester Royals.

New York guard Carl Braun, *center*, attempts a tough shot against the Minneapolis Lakers.

The Knicks rallied to force Game 7. But the Royals held off New York's second-half comeback to win 79–75.

It was the first of three straight Finals losses for the Knicks. The next two came at the hands of the powerhouse Minneapolis Lakers. New York was one of the NBA's best teams in its early years, but it had nothing to show for that success.

KNICKERBOCKER GLORY

The early Knicks had stars like guards Carl Braun and Dick McGuire and forward Harry Gallatin. But as those players grew older and moved on, replacements were tough to find. As a result, the Knicks watched rivals like the Boston Celtics win title after title. Starting in 1956–57, New York's team started a 10-year stretch with only one playoff appearance. Braun and Gallatin even tried to come back and coach the team. Each lasted less than two seasons. Braun went 40–87. Gallatin finished 25–38.

In November 1965, McGuire took over for Gallatin. He also lost more games than he won, but he led the Knicks back to the playoffs a season later. By now, a new crop of stars was emerging. Forward/center Willis Reed led the way, along with forward Bill Bradley, point guard Walt "Clyde" Frazier, and power forward Dave DeBusschere.

It all came together in 1969–70. Under head coach Red Holzman, the Knicks finished the year 60–22. They won the Eastern Division for the first time since 1953–54.

Unlike the teams of the early 1950s, New York finished the job in the 1970 playoffs. Even an injury to Reed in Game 5 of the Finals against the Los Angeles Lakers couldn't hold New York back. The Knicks were finally champions.

The Knicks and Lakers went back to the Finals again two years later. This time Los Angeles won in five games. But New York won 4–1 when the two teams faced off in the Finals again in 1973. Reed had been hobbled by injuries for years but was named Most Valuable Player (MVP) for his inspired play.

That season proved to be the end of the Knicks' short dynasty. Reed retired and briefly became head coach, replacing

From left: Dick Barnett, Walt Frazier, Bill Bradley, Dave DeBusschere, and Willis Reed celebrate the Knicks' 1970 championship.

Holzman in 1977. Holzman took the job back early in the 1978–79 season. He lasted until 1982, but it didn't matter. The Knicks were once again losing more games than they won.

PLAYING THE LOTTERY

By 1984–85 the bottom had come out in New York. The Knicks finished that season 24–58. That summer the NBA was trying a new way to determine the top pick in the draft. The teams that missed the playoffs were entered into a lottery.

The prize that year was a big one. Center Patrick Ewing was a 7-foot, 240-pound star from Georgetown University. He was considered a sure thing for the NBA. League commissioner David Stern reached into a drum containing several envelopes.

The arrival of Patrick Ewing in 1985 helped make New York a contender again.

He pulled out the New York Knicks card. Ewing was coming to the Big Apple.

The lucky break turned the Knicks around. Ewing was a force. He made the All-Star team in 11 of his first 12 seasons. By 1988–89 the Knicks were a playoff regular again. That year they won 52 games.

Three years later, they picked up another legendary head coach. Pat Riley had led the Lakers to four titles in the 1980s. But in 1992–93 the Knicks brought the Schenectady, New York, native closer to home. Riley's Knicks teams were known for both winning games and playing physical defense. New York pummeled any opponent who dared drive to the basket. That defensive style made the Knicks frequent contenders in the 1990s.

BELOW THE SUMMIT

The 1990s were a bad time to be a good NBA team. The league was dominated by superstar guard Michael Jordan and the Chicago Bulls. The Bulls ended New York's season in 1992 and 1993. In 1993 Jordan briefly retired to try playing professional baseball. The Knicks took the opening and reached the NBA Finals. There they lost in seven games to superstar center Hakeem Olajuwon and the Houston Rockets.

Knicks forward Latrell Sprewell attempts a reverse layup during the 1999 NBA Finals against the San Antonio Spurs.

By 1995–96 Jordan was back, and the Bulls went right back to the top. Once again, they ended New York's season in the playoffs. The Knicks won 57 games in 1996–97 but were stopped in the playoffs by a Miami Heat team that was now coached by Riley.

In 1998–99 the NBA season was shortened to 50 games due to a lockout. The Knicks finished 27–23, barely good enough to get into the playoffs. But they upset three higher-seeded teams and reached the Finals. There, the underdog Knicks came up short once again. They lost a five-game series to the San Antonio Spurs.

As the 1999–2000 season came to a close, Ewing was 37 years old. That offseason he left the team. At the time, he owned nearly every franchise record. Coach Jeff Van Gundy tried to keep New York afloat behind solid players like guard Allan Houston and forward Larry Johnson. But the Knicks were out of the playoffs two years later, and Van Gundy resigned.

THE WAY BACK

In the 2000s, the Knicks became known for taking on high-priced players and coaches. But year after year, the moves did not work out. From 2001–02 to 2019–20, the Knicks produced only three winning seasons. The best came in 2012–13. Led by small forward Carmelo Anthony, the Knicks won 54 games. They surprised the league by winning the Atlantic Division. Then they knocked off their longtime rivals, the Boston Celtics, in the first round of the playoffs.

Instead of springing New York to another round of success, the team fell apart due to injuries and inconsistent play. In 2014–15 the Knicks finished 17–65, the worst record in team

RJ Barrett averaged 14.3 points per game as a 19-year-old rookie in 2019–20.

history. Even Phil Jackson, the former Knicks player and 11-time NBA champion coach, couldn't turn things around. Jackson was hired as president of basketball operations in 2014. In four years under his watch, the team went 117–211.

By 2020–21 the Knicks had a pair of talented young players in power forward Julius Randle and shooting guard RJ Barrett. The team brought in Tom Thibodeau to coach them. Most fans expected the young team would take some time to grow into winners. Instead, the Knicks finished 41–31. That was an improvement of 20 wins over the season before. The Knicks' season ended with a loss to the Atlanta Hawks in the opening round of the playoffs. But the team had provided hope that better days were ahead.

CHAPTER THREE

BIG APPLE BALLERS

The first plane ride Harry Gallatin ever took was the one that brought him to New York to play for the Knicks. But the Illinois farm boy wasn't intimidated by his big-city surroundings. The 6-foot-6-inch forward became a seven-time All-Star before leaving the team in 1957.

While Gallatin was from the Midwest, most of the Knicks' early stars were New York products. The team's first point guard, Leo Gottlieb, was from the Bronx. When the Knicks were contending for titles in the early 1950s, they had many local stars. Guard Dick McGuire was a college star at St. John's University in Queens before he became the Knicks' engine. Shooting guard Carl Braun was born in Brooklyn and raised on Long Island.

Harry Gallatin spent nine seasons with the Knicks as a player in the 1940s and 1950s, then coached New York for parts of two seasons in the 1960s.

25

In a way, the sweet-shooting Braun is responsible for one of basketball's most famous terms. Knicks radio announcer Marty Glickman used to say "swish" on broadcasts, after the sound of a ball hitting the net. When the term took off, Glickman was asked where he got the idea. The announcer said he had heard Braun saying it to himself whenever the guard made a shot in warm-ups.

Sweetwater

Until 1950, teams in the BAA/NBA did not allow Black players to compete. Starting with the 1950–51 season, the Knicks helped change that. The team signed forward Nat "Sweetwater" Clifton, who had been playing with the Harlem Globetrotters. Clifton was one of three Black players to enter the league that year. The others were Chuck Cooper of the Boston Celtics and Earl Lloyd of the Washington Capitols. Clifton played seven seasons with the Knicks and made the All-Star team in 1956–57.

BUILDING A DYNASTY

Stars like high-scoring guard Richie Guerin kept the Knicks afloat during the 1960s. But the team didn't win much until Willis Reed came to town. In an era of dominant big men, Reed stood out by being a small center. He was only 6 feet, 9 inches tall. That didn't stop him from earning All-Star honors during his first seven seasons. Reed used his 235-pound frame to bully players down low.

Reed's arrival also signaled the start of what became the

Knicks' golden era. A year later, New York picked up small forward Bill Bradley from Princeton University in the first round. The Knicks also traded for shooting guard Dick Barnett from the Los Angeles Lakers. The 1967 draft brought stellar point guard Walt Frazier. One final deal brought in power forward Dave DeBusschere from the Detroit Pistons.

Willis Reed (19) averaged a double-double in each of his first seven NBA seasons.

By 1969–70 all the pieces were in place. That starting five carried the Knicks to their first NBA title. Frazier dazzled fans at Madison Square Garden with his playmaking ability. He was also New York's second-leading scorer behind Reed. Barnett's sweet shot kept defenses from double-teaming the Knicks' post players. Bradley was both a good scorer and an effective passer. And both Reed and DeBusschere averaged double-doubles in the paint.

The team was led by coach Red Holzman. He had been a player on the Rochester Royals team that beat New York in the 1951 Finals. But on the Knicks' bench, he turned the long-suffering team into a winner. Holzman coached New

York for 14 seasons over two different stints. His 613 wins, nine playoff appearances, and 54 playoff victories are all Knicks records.

By the time the Knicks won again in 1973, a mix of new and old faces were leading the way. Frazier was the team's leading scorer. DeBusschere and Bradley were both still effective stars. But Reed was 30 and battling injuries. That season was his last full year in the NBA.

Barnett was 36 years old and had been reduced to a bench player. The Knicks slotted veteran guard Earl "the Pearl" Monroe into Barnett's spot. Like his nickname, Monroe was one of the flashiest players of his era. When he was traded to the Knicks, many wondered whether his schoolyard style would fit in. The Knicks were known as a disciplined team.

NBA observers also wondered whether Monroe and Frazier could play well together. Both were better when they controlled the ball. But the pairing worked like a charm. In the clinching Game 5 of the

Red Teaches a Legend

One of the Knicks' key reserves in the 1970s was a tall, gangly forward named Phil Jackson. Knicks coach Red Holzman suggested Jackson take up coaching after he retired. Jackson took Holzman's advice. He earned his first head coaching job with the Chicago Bulls in 1989. By the time he left coaching, Jackson had won 11 NBA titles. During four of those title runs, Jackson's Bulls knocked the Knicks out of the playoffs.

Walt Frazier, *right*, was a mainstay in the Knicks' backcourt during the team's success in the late 1960s and early 1970s.

NBA Finals that season, Frazier fed Monroe for a team-high 23 points.

NO LAYUPS

Patrick Ewing was always a player everyone wanted. The towering center was recruited by every top college program when he was in high school in Boston. In 1985 he was coming

Led by head coach Pat Riley, *left*, **and center Patrick Ewing,** *right*, **the Knicks were a bruising opponent in the early 1990s.**

out of Georgetown University, and every NBA team wanted him too.

It wasn't hard to see why. Ewing was 7 feet tall with quick feet and a soft touch around the basket. On defense, his massive hands didn't just block shots but swallowed them up.

The Knicks won the NBA's first draft lottery in 1985. This landed the team its most accomplished player of all time. Ewing left the Knicks in 2000 after destroying nearly every record the team had. His 23,665 points are more than 9,000 ahead of Frazier in second place. Ewing also holds Knicks records for rebounds, blocks, and steals. And he is the only Knicks player to appear in more than 1,000 games.

The only thing Ewing never delivered was a title. His Knicks were a playoff force throughout the late 1980s and 1990s. But they had the bad luck of going up against some of the best NBA teams ever. That didn't stop the Knicks from making opponents suffer to beat them.

Carmelo Anthony was an All-Star in each of his seven seasons with New York.

Under coach Pat Riley in the early 1990s, the Knicks were known for their punishing defense. Ewing teamed up with power forwards Charles Oakley and Anthony Mason. Together, the trio made opponents pay for driving to the basket. Riley's Knicks refused to let opponents have easy layups. On offense, undersized guard John Starks provided hustle and outside shooting.

As the Knicks stayed in contention in the early 2000s, a new crop of stars turned up. Forward Larry Johnson came over in a trade from the Charlotte Hornets in 1996. He helped the Knicks get back to the Finals in 1999. High-scoring guards Latrell Sprewell and Allan Houston also paced the scoring.

MODERN KNICKS

New York has always loved a star. And the Knicks got one in 2011 when forward Carmelo Anthony came to town. Anthony had been one of the best shooters in the NBA since he joined the league in 2003. Two years after arriving in New York, he led the NBA in scoring. He was just the second Knick ever to do that, after Bernard King in 1984–85.

Anthony left the Knicks in 2017 after winning just one playoff series, however. New York was floundering and needed new life. The team got it from a pair of young players. Power forward Julius Randle struggled early in his career with the Lakers. But he broke out with the New Orleans Pelicans in 2018–19. The next summer, the Knicks signed him as a free agent. He made his first All-Star team in 2020–21 while leading New York back to the playoffs.

The Knicks selected RJ Barrett with the third overall pick in the 2019 NBA Draft. The swingman jumped right into the starting lineup and provided reliable scoring. For the first time in nearly two decades, New York had a young core ready to lead the way back to the top.

Julius Randle made the All-NBA second team in 2020–21. He was also the league's Most Improved Player.

CHAPTER FOUR

NEW YORK MOMENTS

The Knicks lost in three consecutive NBA Finals in the 1950s. Two of those losses came to the Minneapolis Lakers. The teams met for the title again in 1970, though the Lakers were now in Los Angeles. Heading into Game 7, it looked as if they might have the Knicks' number this time as well.

The series was tied 2–2 when disaster struck for New York. Center Willis Reed had been the league MVP that year. But he limped off after just eight minutes of Game 5 with a torn thigh muscle. Still, New York held on to win. That put the Knicks just one victory from a title. But without the team's star, many wondered if New York could compete. That looked even less likely when Lakers center Wilt Chamberlain blazed through the Knicks' backup centers for 45 points and 27 rebounds in Game 6.

Willis Reed, *right*, and the Los Angeles Lakers' Wilt Chamberlain, *left*, squared off in the 1970 NBA Finals.

Game 7 was back at Madison Square Garden. The fans who arrived early to watch the teams warm up soon got a surprise. Everyone's attention went to the players' tunnel. Television commentator Jack Twyman was in the middle of his pregame analysis when he suddenly stopped. "I think we see Willis coming out!" Twyman famously shouted.

Sure enough, Reed, his right leg heavily wrapped, was limping onto the court. The New York crowd erupted with hope. So did the big center's teammates. "When I saw that," point guard Walt Frazier later said, "something told me we might have these guys."

Reed could barely move, let alone play. But he hit his first two shots, and the crowd continued to roar. Those proved to be Reed's only points. But his presence inspired the Knicks to a 113–99 win in one of the NBA's most famous games.

Oddly, the real star that night was Frazier. The point guard delivered 36 points and 19 assists. But Game 7 will always be remembered as "the Willis Reed Game."

Reed Runs It Back

Three years after the Willis Reed Game, the Knicks and Lakers met in the Finals again. This time, a healthy Reed spelled quick doom for Los Angeles. The Knicks routed the Lakers in five games. Reed finished off an MVP performance with 18 points, 12 rebounds, and seven assists in Game 5 as the Knicks won their second title.

RIVALRY NIGHTS

New York won a lot of games in the 1990s. But the team's physical brand of basketball didn't make a lot of friends. During the decade, the Knicks had heated rivalries with the Chicago Bulls, Indiana Pacers, and Miami Heat in particular.

Allan Houston celebrates his game-winning shot in Game 5 of the 1999 playoffs against the Miami Heat.

The Knicks and Heat met in the opening round of the playoffs for three straight years. In 1997 and 1998, brawls had overshadowed the play on the court. The teams despised each other by their third meeting, in 1999.

The Heat were heavy favorites. The Knicks had snuck into the playoffs as the eighth seed. At the time, an eighth seed had only ever beaten a top seed once in NBA history. Opening-round playoff series in that era were best-of-five games. The Knicks and Heat went down to the wire in the decisive fifth game.

A steal in the final seconds set New York up with a chance, down by one. After a timeout, New York guard Allan Houston caught an inbounds pass from Charlie Ward. Houston sliced

Larry Johnson had a season-high 26 points in his memorable performance against the Indiana Pacers in Game 3 of the 1999 Eastern Conference finals.

through the middle and hoisted a running jumper from the free-throw line with one second left. The shot bounced off the front rim, up off the backboard, and dropped in. The last-second shot shocked the Miami crowd.

The Knicks faced another rival in the Eastern Conference finals. The Knicks and Pacers were meeting in the playoffs for the fifth time since 1993. In 1995 Pacers star Reggie Miller had stunned New York by scoring eight points in nine seconds late in the fourth quarter of an Indiana win. Now it was time for the Knicks to return that favor.

The series was tied 1–1. With five seconds left in Game 3, the Knicks had the ball down 91–88. Forward Larry Johnson squared up to Indiana defender Antonio Davis at the three-point line. As Johnson took his shot, Davis brushed the Knicks star's right arm. The whistle blew for a foul as the shot dropped in. Johnson briefly celebrated, then calmed down to sink the foul shot. The miracle four-point play held up when Indiana guard Mark Jackson missed a shot at the buzzer. The Knicks went on to win the series in six games to return to the NBA Finals.

LINSANITY

The Knicks didn't make many playoff memories in the 2010s. But they did provide one of the most thrilling stretches of regular-season basketball the NBA has ever seen. It was all thanks to a little-known point guard who became famous overnight.

Jeremy Lin was not expected to make it in the NBA. By the time he joined the Knicks in late 2011, he had already been cut by two teams. He had barely played for New York by the end of January 2012. The Knicks were ready to cut him again. He caught a break only when all of the team's other point guards

Almost History

In the 1951 NBA Finals, the Knicks nearly pulled off a stunning comeback. After falling behind 3–0 to the Rochester Royals, the Knicks won the next three games to force a decisive Game 7. Rochester recovered to win the series after taking the final game 79–75. It took another 43 years after the Knicks did it until the 1994 Denver Nuggets forced a Game 7 after trailing 3–0. However, no NBA team has ever come back from 3–0 down to win a series.

were injured. New York was struggling as well at 8–15.

On February 4, the Knicks faced the New Jersey Nets. Lin shone off the bench, scoring 25 points in a Knicks win. Knicks head coach Mike D'Antoni decided to keep him in the lineup.

The Knicks rattled off six more wins after Lin was named the starter. He was the star of the show. Against the Lakers, he outscored superstar guard Kobe Bryant in another victory.

On Valentine's Day, Lin hit a buzzer-beating three-pointer in a 90–87 win over the Toronto Raptors. After the shot, the term "Linsanity" was introduced to describe what fans were seeing. In two weeks, Lin had gone from nearly out of the league to its newest star.

Lin even gained an invitation to the Rising Stars game at All-Star weekend. At the time, he had started just 11 games. A month later, Lin suffered a knee injury that kept him out the rest of the regular season. The Knicks went 15–10 in Lin's 25 starts, turning their season around to finish 36–30.

Jeremy Lin, *left*, is congratulated by teammates after hitting his game-winning shot against the Toronto Raptors on February 14, 2012.

After the season, Lin left the Knicks and signed with the Houston Rockets. He never played for New York again, leaving the legend of "Linsanity" intact forever.

TIMELINE

1946
The Knickerbockers begin play in the BAA.

1949
The Knicks become an original NBA team when the BAA merges with the National Basketball League.

1951
The Knicks rally from 3–0 down in the NBA Finals before losing in seven games to the Rochester Royals.

1953
The Knicks lose in the NBA Finals to the Minneapolis Lakers. It's New York's third Finals loss in as many years.

1964
The Knicks select Willis Reed in the second round of the NBA Draft.

1970
Led by an MVP performance from Reed and Walt Frazier's 36 points in Game 7, the Knicks win their first NBA championship by defeating the Los Angeles Lakers.

1972
New York falls to the Lakers in a five-game NBA Finals.

1973
The Knicks win their second NBA title by routing the Lakers in five games.

1985
The Knicks win the first NBA Draft lottery and select center Patrick Ewing with the top pick.

1994
New York reaches the NBA Finals for the first time in 21 years but loses in seven games to the Houston Rockets.

1999
Allan Houston's buzzer-beater in the first round against the Miami Heat and Larry Johnson's four-point play in Game 3 of the Eastern Conference finals help the Knicks reach the NBA Finals for the eighth time in team history.

2013
The Knicks finish 54–28 and claim their first division title since 1993–94.

2019
New York signs Julius Randle as a free agent and drafts RJ Barrett third overall.

2021
The Knicks reach the playoffs for the first time in eight years but fall 4–1 in the first round to the Atlanta Hawks.

TEAM FACTS

FRANCHISE HISTORY
New York Knickerbockers
(1946–)

NBA CHAMPIONSHIPS
1970, 1973

KEY PLAYERS
Carmelo Anthony (2011–17)
RJ Barrett (2019–)
Bill Bradley (1967–77)
Carl Braun (1947–50, 1952–61)
Dave DeBusschere (1968–74)
Patrick Ewing (1985–2000)
Walt Frazier (1967–77)
Harry Gallatin (1948–57)
Allan Houston (1996–2005)
Charles Oakley (1988–98)
Julius Randle (2019–)
Willis Reed (1964–74)
John Starks (1990–98)

KEY COACHES
Red Holzman (1967–77, 1978–82)
Joe Lapchick (1947–56)
Pat Riley (1991–95)

HOME ARENAS
69th Regiment Armory (1946–60)
Madison Square Garden III (1946–68)
Madison Square Garden IV (1968–)

TEAM TRIVIA

THE FIRST OF MANY

The Knicks played in the first game in NBA history on November 1, 1946. They traveled to play the Toronto Huskies and emerged with a 68–66 victory.

SENATOR BRADLEY

After winning two NBA titles with the Knicks, Bill Bradley was elected to the United States Senate in 1979. He served three terms in the Senate before leaving in 1997. Bradley attempted to run for President in 2000 but lost the Democratic nomination to Al Gore.

THE ORIGINALS

The NBA had 17 teams in its first season. But only two were still playing in their original cities in 2021–22—the Knicks and the Boston Celtics. The longtime rivals met in 14 postseason series, with each team winning seven series.

THE STYLE OF CLYDE

Walt "Clyde" Frazier was one of the NBA's first style icons. He was known for his loud suits, gold chains, and turtlenecks. His fashion sense even created his nickname, "Clyde." After he wore wide-brimmed hats as a young player, Knicks trainer Danny Whelan gave him the name as a reference to Warren Beatty's outlaw character in the film *Bonnie and Clyde*.

GLOSSARY

assist
A pass that leads directly to a basket.

capacity
The maximum number of fans an arena or stadium can hold.

contender
A person or team that has a good chance at winning a championship.

double-double
Accumulating 10 or more of two certain statistics in a game.

draft
A system that allows teams to acquire new players coming into a league.

lockout
A work stoppage during which owners bar the players from playing or practicing.

rebound
To catch the ball after a shot has been missed.

resigned
Quit one's job.

rival
An opponent with whom a player or team has a fierce and ongoing competition.

steal
To take the ball from a player on the other team.

triple-double
Accumulating 10 or more of three certain statistics in a game.

MORE INFORMATION

BOOKS

Flynn, Brendan. *The NBA Encyclopedia for Kids*. Minneapolis, MN: Abdo Publishing, 2022.

Mahoney, Brian. *GOATs of Basketball*. Minneapolis, MN: Abdo Publishing, 2022.

Ybarra, Andres. *Great Basketball Debates*. Minneapolis, MN: Abdo Publishing, 2019.

ONLINE RESOURCES

To learn more about the New York Knicks, please visit **abdobooklinks.com** or scan this QR code. These links are routinely monitored and updated to provide the most current information available.

INDEX

Anthony, Carmelo, 22, 32

Barnett, Dick, 27–28
Barrett, RJ, 8, 23, 32
Bradley, Bill, 18, 27–28
Braun, Carl, 17–18, 25–26

Chamberlain, Wilt, 35
Clifton, Nat, 26

D'Antoni, Mike, 40
DeBusschere, Dave, 18, 27–28

Ewing, Patrick, 19–20, 22, 29–31

Frazier, Walt, 18, 27–30, 36

Gallatin, Harry, 17–18, 25
Glickman, Marty, 26
Gottlieb, Leo, 25
Guerin, Richie, 26

Holzman, Red, 18–19, 27, 28
Houston, Allan, 22, 32, 37–38

Jackson, Mark, 39
Jackson, Phil, 23, 28
Johnson, Larry, 22, 31, 39
Jordan, Michael, 10, 21

Kase, Max, 15
King, Bernard, 32

Lapchick, Joe, 17
Lee, Spike, 9–10
Lin, Jeremy, 39–41

Mason, Anthony, 31
McGuire, Dick, 17–18, 25
Miller, Reggie, 10, 38–39
Monroe, Earl, 28–29

Oakley, Charles, 31

Pippen, Scottie, 10

Randle, Julius, 8–9, 11–12, 23, 32
Reed, Willis, 18, 26–28, 35–36
Riley, Pat, 11, 20–21, 31
Rose, Derrick, 11

Sprewell, Latrell, 32
Starks, John, 31

Thibodeau, Tom, 9, 11, 23

Van Gundy, Jeff, 22

Ward, Charlie, 37

Young, Trae, 9–12

ABOUT THE AUTHOR

Anthony K. Hewson is a freelance writer originally from San Diego. He and his wife now live in the San Francisco Bay Area with their two dogs.